I0876684

PRIOR PRAISE FOR JENNY GRASSL

"With a flicker of Brock-Broido and a fringe of Dickinson, Grassl swims us through an ornate up-river so that we react perhaps with heart, instead of head, with gut and also god."

—Jennifer Militello, author of *Identifying the Pathogen*

"[T]here is a syllabic ecstasy mirroring that of the night sky and starlight. Echoic in their magic, these poems answer fact with fable and ephemera with deeply rooted imagery and home truths. Grassi knows the uses of enchantment, and she uses it deftly and delightfully."

—Donald Revell, author of *Canandaiuga*

"This is pastoral dipped in fire and swelling with song, an immersive experience unlike in any poetry currently popular. This is Grassl's world, unmistakable and riveting."

—Joan Houlihan, author of *It Isn't a Ghost if it Lives in Your Chest*

"Deploying associative images and white space on the page, each line is spell casting—"

—Robert Carr, author of *The Heavy of Human Clouds*

FOREVER MISTAKEN FOR OURSELVES

JENNY GRASSL

Forever Mistaken For Ourselves

ISBN: 978-1-961209-71-8

Cover and text design by Allison O'Keefe

Front cover: Cover artwork is an original woodcut collaboration by Jenny and Anton Grassl. Jenny drew the image on a woodblock, and Anton carved it. Used by permission.

First paperback edition: Deccember 2026

Tupelo Press

P.O. Box 1767

North Adams, Massachusetts 01247

(413) 664-9611 / Fax: (413) 664-9711

editor@tupelopress.org / www.tupelopress.org

Tupelo Press is an award-winning independent literary press that publishes fine fiction, non-fiction, and poetry in books that are a joy to hold as well as read. Tupelo Press is a registered 501(c)(3) nonprofit organization, and we rely on public support to carry out our mission of publishing extraordinary work that may be outside the realm of the large commercial publishers. Financial donations are welcome and are tax deductible.

FOREVER MISTAKEN FOR OURSELVES

JENNY GRASSL

Tupelo Press
North Adams, Massachusetts

CONTENT

III. TRYING ON THE GARDEN

IV. SMOKE AND SHELTER

In those days the world of mirrors and the world of men were not, as they are now, cut off from each other. They were, besides, quite different; neither beings nor colors nor shapes were the same. Both kingdoms, the specular and the human, lived in harmony; you could come and go through mirrors. One night, however, the people of the mirror invaded this world.

—Jorge Luis Borges, *Imaginary Beasts*

A Wounded deer–leaps highest–

—Emily Dickinson

I.

SKINS OF THE ELEMENTS

IRON DRESSES

late in the age of lightening
when heavy came up for air
made mostly of air

I choose one ferrous dress   late
in my age   a faulty
armor will do
Anthropocene-erotic
fitted bell
dinosaur caged rib
and farthingale

I have to be poured in   like a resin reeking of forest
I do not leak   carrying myself

but who am I   camouflaged
to transparence

is it the gods who grant me steel now
to more lightly stride a road cut into the hill   high tension
power-line new   unbound from iron molecule

towers land   giantess dresses forcing clouds
a fleet of sisters
old corsets buckling into powder rust
we are high voltage pylons strong

forever mistaken for ourselves

DEER WOMAN IN THE DINING ROOM

antlers bud blood-pink   twelve points

rise with woman pain   always the escaped

smell of iron and shame   I stain

serve sore at table in apron whites   pour wine

fork meat   diners finger silver

knives around this heartbeat   centerpiece

of one's own rack thorned and tender

the curious read my roses there

a dozen   tines hardened

one for each lunar month   each apostle

each egg in a box   a bone curl for each step of away

from a lush life   when sheet ghosts wilt

down to milk of All Souls' Day

mortal most   scarlet

injury   jackstraw arrows fly at my

cry-alive   and God

says *Praise me*

IN A TIME OF EXTINCTION

speak of me in a coal clean burn of your furnished heart

and say   how   you might find my body   terraqueous

bone in water   humid eye in socket   I am a sea

of castaways   a flotsam of outfits to hold a day's skin

tell how I float an ark of the only one   of each kind

through cracks in the city   my tissue trembles like a peony as if

goodbye   a tattoo never suffered cannot sink

your name   where   in a channel my veins could loosen

to the tide   exacted   by gull and ghost crab   I'd have

your oxygen   deep   and this would be known as love

of each outgrown skeleton   yours   mine   the longer

bones   now the porous and honeyless combed   laying

down fossils in sandbar or seep   scratched to the child

THE PRIMAL ACCIDENT

gurgling up from the bridge of them   overlanded
flood child of Skipback Creek   their north/south kiss
sleet and peach   in my throat   I spoke from a widowed place
of love   changing hands   child   to favored child
a failure of the woods to raise me to a supper table   shining
sticky haloed when I played dead   mirror switched with love
my prizes   to nourish like the back of an envelope licked
dear boyfriends   I did not mean to bring you   to this want

WOMAN'S *MAPPA MUNDI*— THE PROMONTORY IMPRINT

a bubbling gone rogue

my song summons hounds of heaven
there are no sailors
to risk sirens
sea pig rides the waves

my lap subsumes
blood chambers of the deep

fins of all the fathers   a dead man's float

cracked and crashed by a shopping cart
ship mast skews vertebrae in a puddle

gone   the tide   littoral long dead

surf pulls weak   dumps old tools for the merman feast
knife shucks open   woman I could be

tiny pearl to steer by
clenched between fish scale hips

unhoused and flipped
flesh against stone—

a mermaid prone—

HOLES IN THE WIND

unhinged first
from last
name named wherefore does it pour

why are you
you each cell holds the lion's paw
alabaster alphabet
gusty helix pair and drosophila

the body bends with asphodel
backbone pearled
earth-and-sky-bowed to adore
infinitude—so few years back a love

every poem is a Sappho fragment
of some poor cloth
shawl we shiver in

all our words what we really mean

every gap in a Sappho poem an epic

QUEEN ANNE'S BLACK LACE

a dress is a door you slam shut   by opening cloth softly   a long row
of buttonholes slipping your love   to a man   who was after your dress
in its cloud of ambergris   and deeply pleasured leanings toward good
are you done with skirts' false meadow   and the long coat of his night
swell with your breasts alone   in a field   where grasshopper zither
dies back in singe   you   an ecstatic   burn pagan fevers   in shin bone
and wrist   split into grass nerve   wild rye and goldenrod whip
your stride   limbs burst yellow   tasseled in bracts of autumn mutiny
rolls of slow brown stars prickle in wool   your dress dies in a swath
of broken orbits and outfits   *Rudbeckia* petals   and lupine
dropped back to wolf   wild carrot draws a map of the soot
and bloom of you   blackening the lace   holes you leave open for the ghosts

HEM OF FIRE

you ran from lava licks

the women saved you

bits of tulle and lawn
clippings   from their pots

moss and talk to grow your gown

how you wore bride   wife   mother

swore years of velvet sage
and common sooty wing
of a dragged butterfly
they let you go
when their apples filled with wasps

you landing in vines and looped loves
naked in your name

fumbling with veils

nailing
the immortal weeds

and lace of last frost
to the hourglass

couldn't they command more
                    bring a fist of horsemint
cradling from the grave

HUMAN

sapiens scent comes troubling
into spirit hollow of vena cava
heart of the deer

her body gods
what of roadkill

adrenaline-run   the herd flees
to other caves   Lascaux
or the purple-lit Endless Caverns

amygdala   hair-triggers fear or any gala

man-scared pathways lead in all directions
blood thickets in winter   bird-clutched and berry red
antler crowned   she cannot extricate plume of her human

bucks bear oracle breath
branching from interior lace

of islands and frozen lakes ossifying

overhead

they clash for sex and land force helixes of dawn

to a velvet spring

she does not wonder past the road

and deer do not graze to the known

edge of grief

all the kingdoms of horizons belong

to fenced yard the does in the field

wading in star grass

to the underside of visible

she lies down not knowing by the drawn bow shade

call it a great love

II.

BEASTS LIVING IN THE MIRROR

BEASTS LIVING IN THE MIRROR

could not be banished
silvering behind double cross
mock to meet all gaze and ways   a little off

who will feed or starve their caves of want

my eyes are slaves
to these animals

one half-man fish thwacks free   breaking glass   splash out of a looking
whole body kiss   pushes me into reflection he has been

zoo-seething jar
a reckoning

now comb your hair   rouge your lips
from the other side   through a darkly   woman   what do you see

you polishing your fish scales
admiring shine I will blunt
with my breath
you become like me before I was reversed
in thrall—
your eyes—

DIARY OF DEER WOMAN

over a bed preened to swallow

living bodies of ghost-fit   a visit of catastrophes

I spread brown velvet
dredged   shined

my antlers reach too high for me to rest my head

I vanish with a hound

hunted imprints with hunter

phantom archers will tell you how sweet

among the succulents

to browse by night

my husband can't sleep here   the antlers disarrange him

the screech of the howlers swinging from tine to tine

{{ { { { { { { { { {

GRACE

angels strip   the harp cascading

turn   into deer   where you live

in your servant skins   mystic with a broom

the thought   of the hunted day   being not day

but all days   or camellias   or their hole

in the buck   bloomed at the arrow

meat on the laid low table   a Most Wanted

carpenter long dead   bowing to your meal

REAP IN THUNDER LONG

she   masterfully in the mirror

wakes   some reassurance

of a hereafter   requiring a here

if she is   a silver say-so   dawn fog

stumbles her get-go   tiptoe into dirt

off the plotted beds   the halving wound

a vague sweet   petal blouse lift

she   bare-breasted to the hoverfly shimmer

mallow a-wrestle   with spoke of thistle

in the meadow   her rose nipple hardens

REFLECTION AS BEING IN LOST HABITAT

to be so double

in deep mirror of the open

land

to be now fused with hum and harrow

to be rose mallow   merged

into radial pinks   the blood-blind center

of the world   flower of mobbed stigmata

to become wide   greedy green

with the lawn and its leaned

lethargies

to have been like that once

from comfort into strain

lines in the looking glass follow   field furrow

distorted in a gown   I am placed in the new-ripe

to have reflex

be meadow mowed down to pores

cross herd nibble   grub grass of glory's demise

all will be

like dew   frost-killed and kept

venison wrapped in paper

white as the dress

to give oneself in

bold

where the dog flushes rabbits

brush cover undone

to be holding upright then the cup   a tiny hemlock drop

summer curtsied for the turn

TO THE ANIMALS DREAMING MY BODY

in my purse must be a horse
if stag sleeps in ash tree

cricket rubs off-tempo
loud in a rib cage hush

no summer cup weep   only see

cattle crowd to drink my eyes
at edge

hear
at keyhole ear
whitewater want

feel   the wilding

haunch lost with ox
when skin turns home to exile

years until I tongue the wolves

an owl mantling

COMING INTO HOOVES

while morning coffee roams to everlasting
cup of want dis-timely   not fixed in when
four ebony keys' hammers hit strings
paired cloven song   deer play on dewclaws
spied under the hem of a resting cloud tableau
beneath my feet woodgrain sweats
shoes not slick as hoof   I kick them off
craving tough   to create heat   a keratin
flow surround   toes fuse and harden
cramp   fully ungulate   I run through
brambled lots of gravel   a leap of lack
street clack to concrete-held roofs   scrape
my rack of bone on dragon or demon stone
grimaces   down to what's velvet and possible

HOW YOU GET BACK HOME

seek preternature

of the woods   the light short

like cake   long

on butter   and going

fast

moss soft in its crypt of rock   crevassed

to get there   a rocking horse

an offer of wooden apples

follow the crack   widening

ride into perforated shade spangling

acquire crow gleam before dark

land on your porch   crescendo rising

breaching walls and open doors

the repeat   of a man's Wagner heart

drags cricket song

your winged Valkyries' ride

song of women not trifling

choosing the dead   for a heaven

you know you could   but he owns the sound

watch through rusted screens

because you always wandered off

you must carry a tender ruin

HOOVES

trailing archipelago of a dress

run counter canyon to the heart be river and sea

let antlers share halls of moss and staghorn fern
green room to smoke in
before you take the stage
back hooves kick dirt

but can you swim to anyone on dry land
only the departed
bones of a whole
deer laid in a lake given thanks for meat

know this gesture will not save

hoof your hands
grow calluses fill all
palm divining-lines stiff with horn

turn back Darwin's ship

you are almost there
all doe and buck

skin if long and cervine   head high   fear something

you could almost carry a fawn

call for shiver

nuzzle the fir-branched snow

HOW TO GROW COVER

I.

daffodils break stare
body newfangle

I spy a stag through branches

throw wish at his feet
nearing—being—
deer—

how a woman crowned for the hunt too naked for snow bed—
lance and saw-tooth flake
split arcs of storm

I have left the dining room
to land here on four hooves a stammer

II.

mating remembered as late summer
how in his yard how a freeze near death
how an elder silver doe brings attar of compass rose

one drink in spring and I belong

RINGING

every time I make a mark
it makes me

body's thicket of veins
a scroll of plum tree linking continents

my black skirt clouds a puddle on the path

crowd of aspen gazing
cut by knives of sun

each silence vaulting
casts sound shadows in my ears
choirs of monks moaning
in split-interval pitch   beauty of woe
like tinnitus
I am not alone

fruit-greeded   fallow-seeded with mint
eclipse cotton flares in my pocket
waves of entanglement

fever burns below the famine labyrinth
I lose one half and read the sign where I turn
not looking back

and yet return to whole and hatch
and which move moves me
out of place   that I might find

III.

TRYING ON THE GARDEN

WEDDING DRESSES BY ANSELM KIEFER

—buying them—I was asked
do you have a harem

I don't own any nouns
only trace   melt   lace
verbs arrested on the hills
force of a dress
plaster slapped on
wide skirts
hardened to glacier   left in the sun
bridal trains calving   pools of feminine

I did not bleed
them from my loins
machines and industrial strength   sorrow
a kind of borrow
I took
the Chantilly lantern inside each girl
once their only guide

I disembody their gowns
crowned with barbed wire
who owns trauma

but these—
idling through my estate grounds—
I dedicate to the glory of women

of course girls in rooms
mapped the rivers
wet threads to needle
spooling roads to destination of coupling
their wedding dress
kept in the breast
flickers   light
I follow   leaving them behind
snuffed for this fame
folds   who ironed them
rust burns   that kind of irony

VENICE FIGURINE WEDS AFTER SURVIVING A LOST WEDDING

a sea of creatures ago I turn into whitest rock   a woman left and leaving
in the next life I die   absolving ribbons of sleep   boats in the canal
hands pouring Lethe   water taxi glissando   islands burning with glass and lace
swarms of Putti gold struck over earthly   asp at my throat   langostini
tangle of antennae under tourists' forks   why my living abalone heart desired by one
thousand kleptomania eyes   and timorous mouthed reasons to exist   fleshly
darks the marble   Helmut Newton style haircut frames someone like me
to be bereaved   a bleed   for birds who don't care at the spigot
for global givens and takens   I take champagne and cinder capsules
to singe the likeness— sudden tremble   pink palate   and liver-embered ash

MEADOW OF CORSET

lace me   shut
do not stay my desire in velvet gone stiff
love take rescue from the rhizome mat
its death camp mercied underfoot
seeds' odds sad chanced   things are breaking
time pieces of crickets   asters burning
half-lives at yellow centers of pale lavender
the promise of skin   my repair is only to stare
at the turn and tawn of summer   gather
round me   lover leafless   your wane
or rampancy gone strange   solicit more cage
for my long hair   awns and burr stars
clutch and sting my breakdown
dragonfly wafts a trail of blue smoke
last rites through the verticals
pierce all ceremony with arc and landing
of Orthoptera   a spider drops into afterlife
crawl meadow   crawl   how could we
end this multiflora honey with a slow bee

NASTURTIUMS

deep in the flower you coax   feel the pod-throb
like your own pulse   and the vine bluing in your wrist
grow penumbras of spring in hour of ancestor
their amniotic skins shadow and onion-hover you
keeper of the green flame   binge toward peak flowering
let folded-in wings crack and fly   their color stun rip
of red   gold and orange   a pyromania spurred by spice
from earth's core and surface honey   when frost breaks them
at the knees   pull stems away from the ground   by root
and wastrel hair   yanked scaffolding of a summer
hold high the vine soaking your garden gloves
last juice   to shake the earth and inherit

DEAR SURVIVOR

I am beached at the tide of wild
daisy and chthonic stich
of the corn spider   day drawn faster
and grass step-steep in the blue eye hills'
cresting clew   just a dayflower
dwarf in the blur-vast view
by won-heart ingress of loose strife
laced with a century   hence-deep
and yours my heir   once cradled
rocking out of a dawn from where I came

FLOWER OF EMPIRE: The Two-night Life and Sex Change of *Victoria Amazonica*

I astonish in a white dress

my never whole
spectacle woman tough-gloried

out of the shell of spines   a body

in hundreds of pieces   petals arranged
by a god who was sorry
granting beauty opening perfume

attracts the scarab beetle

to pollinate landing in my skirts

petals surround

wonder at my stigma tremble

It is my turn

O how the darkness makes me love the queen

and it should come to this red dress

fallen with morning on my cold shoulders

blades opened for all

man-yellow

anther-freaked

is it any wonder cross-cut halo

nerve   my shadow   revising on a leaf

paint a page of botany before

madness   the soul's exact

fragility

bud bristled and animal—

WHERE DID YOU FLEE WITHOUT A NIGHT

for cover   a shade so handsome

light so broke   in a forest gleamed with ambush

you are one tree on the run

why do I take star leaf from your hem of hex

*

the woodcutter cannot reach
your inner ring   the promise of cake

he tells me   fells me   *you always feel too much*   I slip
away to your rub carnal   no one can see

*

you   black locust shuddered in pollen
and I   woman of deep tissue without skin
a depth you crave
fallen in sweet cicely   henbit and wintergreen

*

where lacewing nymphs move air crumbs
truck fodder under us for mushroom shove   kneading your bast   my flesh   together

kiss dilates my bones   splits your trunk   ways of earth crypt plumb

our hands branching into lichen

*

the truth is   my lying down the north

and south of you divides me

ferrying sugar   water for milk

I climb inside your old crown bell

hunters bagging songbirds

*

men begging to feel their own bodies

turning with the liquid iron center of the earth

if you could grant them

vertigo   sex and snow   one drop of sap

*

what then   stalkers never content at the end

shout *run*   propping you up

felling the clouds

WHO DO YOU LOVE

every heroine needs an adversary
shadow behind to impersonate her light
colonize her colon and salon
invisible legions of suitors and slayers
petaled animal   slithered plant-seeming
viruses recline on couches leave calling cards
cells with outlandish hatted heads tipping
above tentacled skirts   Celtic knots spikes
and whimsy tails   chain link torsos
tent cities flap in the lungs   stars go out
closed in a holy book apocalypse of breath
even the class of *enemy* can turn friend
viral phages eavesdrop   lie in wait
for deadly bacteria to start the party
celebrating successful body takeover
this a signal for the sword   angel phages
kill for the finest feast   save the human
body at thriller's end   shared habitat
shares microbiome   who you love

EARTHLOCK

Atilt, atingle, with load I hide my soul. **B**ottom feeders nose my feet, my sex, **C**omb bones. I crush and seed **D**rupelets of raspberries on my tongue, **E**ked out of ardor, stunning papillae. **F**etch a remedy, a Lord, a father, **G**rouching, historic. **H**arsh, the shape of desire. **I**ce in its clockturn, opaque, the blood rush Jaspered. **J**ust one scrap of planet **K**issed and missed in the snow's descent. **L**ord, the futile lords flee. **M**ake me a hat in a rabbit. Petition. **N**ever too long the wait for salvation. **O** innocent. I was visited, then grew **P**infeathers, beloved on the chick. **Q**uid pro quo. Lethe, please. **R**emember not the old boyfriends **S**unk in my empty hold. Hold me now. **T**hine, the riddle of that. Your revealed **U**pended law of attraction, the ionized mist. **V**ouchsafe the meek the inch, an arch **W**avelength's worm, heart-burrowed. **X**ylem to your name's sake flows. My eyes **Y**ellow irides of cat. I dwell in an eased garden **Z**oo of the prey, wild thistle and loin.

TRANSLATE US

I swallowed a language whole to meet your gaze

and spoke for days things old and navel to the tongue

your meadowy name   of mine   I traded American

swoon-whine   tipped tulip tree   on bedrock shale

we sat high on a pale limestone slope   fanned fires

in the gut with Alpine air   a glacier-cooled speech forged

to build and turn a Fachwerk phrase   toy towns

with Grimm   and sauerkraut steam   where I longed to find

words for things I could not say or mean   mountain river

without a continent   whitewater   talk   sticky   *ich, du*

sumptuous misunderstandings   we left the other side

of an echo   bell-wrung   to need   to woo

NOMENCLATURE

name   their colors and thus command   the overtaking years
at the *frond green* front   a line advancing   on the most fluke

alone   of the first *peeled lime*   of oak leaf tine in spring   winning
darker   dandered in *hawk shade*   profligate   variegate   mixed

with bark weave   known as *army*   camouflage   foliage bored through
by gum resin eye of raptor   *gamboge* above   gathering ray to disclose

nose quiver   at mouse hole   a mile below   like your days made of Now
stalked by the foresight of When   its *wretch-scarlet* let   after the heart's

blue moments of blood   color called *wing feather jay joy*   *tongue bruise*
or *absence of orange in the fruit bowl*   *aphasia clear* descends

so you fill The Forgettery   that *soiled-linen-gray* mausoleum cabinet
in the side of a mountain   with labeled drawers for lost words   and doors

closed on unruly heaps of clothes awaiting sorting   The Month Before X
X With You   The Years After X   name it *feral indigo*   a *clam mud pale*

compartment is filed envelopes   are December   November   March
Before Birth   *Now* thrives   yellow favored as a blonde   cruel as jaundice

builds   with city sirens when temperatures rise   green and blue yield
to its acid and its balm   name it *cinquefoil*   *gallstone*   *racetrack*

peeled paint of a colonial home   until the *then* of night burns
the lamp   of missing light   a hindsight of *Jupiter black*

THE ART OF LOSING SUMMER

blood aligning north

slag-cinnamon and stray

what is August late for

July's ruby voice

gone garnet and gaunt   hearsay-hoarse

September

udder to moon

my weeds are iron

the continent sinks in swimming holes

I can't get to from here

weather is all that is going on

a soul is Labor Day near and ships have sailed

in glances of glass bottling

sand passed   from my hand to a child's

tiny ants set my nerves on filigree fire

with departure   in low sun

prisms will break up night sky I won't see

I am so south

though I might take more

be vulpine   feather-flushed

fox knows mouth feel of waterfowl

he can't eat flock grief whole

or make geese not go

isn't it fine when change wrecks the scene

beautiful stranger   hello

IV.

SMOKE AND SHELTER

DEER WOMAN AS MELPOMENE, FACES THE MANIC COMEDY   : > ((< :

I keep no secret
knowing it myself

wildfire burns the fool
bequeath her skull
lantern to inferno
smell her hair in the hills ignite
long struck lightning of ago

I collect   protect   the nay I say
to grinning smoke

Tube of *Hot Mama Matte* lipstick   does not help

rouged edge of all my excess
comic uptilt   I can never feign a smile

what faces can I know

I lose dreams to newborn mouth an 'O'
hunger waking every day   then O!

sings—
a roll in the blood
surge   into queen

angling to build
monument for always—human husk—
exhumed in profane light two masks

Thalia smiles to view the shiny jungle
braiding out of control
strikes her carefree match

smile or bile
I can still follow
the violin spider
playing her sad octave

nature seen only in a pane of squared-off heat

outdoor pastimes canceled

give the babies TV

why do I not join the shrug or joke
escape myself Melpomene's downsake

the next generation wakes
diaper in the pail kiss on the cheek

IF CREMATION

were a jovial occasion   not mother burn of Canada woods

chain lightning flames run to blue-eyed grass

reaching you   Jove holding you down   wildfire licks

beneath his cloud beard   birds incinerated in the fog

smoke smells like gods like men

lanyards heavy at day's end   glands smirking

what could you take   there will be no posthumous

clothes   oxygen   confused in the particulate

what is kept in the cages with doves on the pyre

the kiss   blue-green world theft

forced by scarlet tongues

your deep-time watch set to walk away

from crackling   remote words   letters on a page—scaffolding

for something you half remember

you and the Earth—old sparks from broke-child rock

if winged horses

if imaginings had to work the line

to survive   here you are in the electrome

going back to fix the fairytales   extinguish the wick to house of char

EROS QUAKE

what feral mountain takes the lion down
                    bluing   covered in snow
to bury bone in a valley home   shadow turn
                              of the sun and its gnomon   cannot keep
                    time with change
                              of heart   range or retreat

ice   rock   mosaic break in hulk   music choking a stream
                    reflecting locks   a woman's hair
currents of her skin   and an unkempt eye

                              which particles cohere into sentiment
                    beneath the peaked   now wrecked
she would carry some goats   once prey   or gods now slit-eyed and stray
                              as she considers the trouble
                    of beginning again   arranging tectonic smoke
around her shoulders

AFTERMATH

the codling moth will overwinter now

let no speech
lend your bruise
fresh colors of the moor
blazon of long gone kin
and your own skin
though woods drop leaf   lace
and ligament to bone
daylight is safe in its extra
hour of wakeless
dusk a sooner dread
chanted in the quire

a Romanesque huddle of vast
the uncandled nerve exposed

blackened nave
cowls the thinning throng
whose wrong childhoods
surface on the platter of the king

LAMPS LIT WITH WANE

tell me what I know

when light tells me to fail

spoons in drawers
hooded   hushed

the table I can't

set

window near me May of months

so squarely brimmed

why let the view out turn moth to stone

pea gravel   glittered hard

what I think I know

old women dwell
where trees were cut

rousing trunks to stride

edges of people bevel toward me

untangling chains
I drape between feather and sky

so tell how to see sleep of rock

say it is dangerous and thrall

beneath cloud slicks the cinder clock

flesh and black daffodil

DEER WOMAN WRITES TO HER CHILDREN

cipher-dark I call   you sing back velvet
                    skipped in moss

          wildcat mint lights your dendritic fires

ferning vast things lost only to me

          you keep no thought bedded like an injured wren on mimosa flowers
I find you free on thunder pauses

          wearing crown lobes of oak   taken off for sleep

no skull writhes raising bone   antlers like mine
          sheltering raptors of pique

          you run toward blackened reams I write
your crowns beam up   meet satellites unblinking

overtones of a lyre I cannot hear

                    who will snuff night to lampblack
                    tree wicks leaning leafless
                    unable to light the winter without clamor

          of child to mother   you cry for strings of colored lights.

ATTEND THE CROWNING HEAD

I will listen lovesick   country   to your rain

                    in the amnion   your sac of ruin

ravens call the caul descending

          I will keep our faces

the ground receives the sunflower roar   a lion bowed

          to shreds of mane

                              while ten thousand children

chime whitely in the sun

                    can we not succumb

the bumblebees hang on gray and quiet   to cosmos' last violet sails

                    will I author us

                              full honey in the hive

in cursive arcs of swarm flight

                    there is no acorn   that believes and knows

HEAVENLY BODY POSTMENOPAUSAL

maybe we've got it wrong   postponing fire   dowsing
the stone   of earth   for whitewater   whelping green and breathe
how breathtaking   last river in estrus   dried   a centipede
seen from above   fern   fen   and fringe   locust and its honey
dripping rest slipped into a planet's thirst   an art   fermata stalks
the roar   when live-born young   licked by mother tongue   die
into the extinct powders   sea sand and chalk   waterless   after stench
for a while   a grimace of upturned stones   perhaps we do
perceive their souls   deeply lapidary   or the pangs of magnetic fields
that outlast a Berlin blue of sky   the maternal gone easily for gravity
rocks a-whirl in what was wet   alive   and we   who did stanch
the animal in our iron-rich hearts   before rust   before slag
and crucible   vanish into the serene void of the father

LAST BLUSH OF MY CHAPPED PLANET

I put it away   it rattled in my custody   it shrank

no live oceans tipping off the ball   no gerrymandered bitters

no grain braiding itself in the wind   no pride of lions

humbling   the view ever   sunk with haloing

of an old lens   no museums to hold the early deaths

no episcopal breath   no bears who dance beyond

their chains   no rivers opening mouths of caves

no karst   no wanderlust   no fern unfurling

the body of a cello   just a bauble made of unfamiliars

a lost kingdom of mine

UNDER TRAVELING WILDFIRE HAZE

I don't wish to kill

just hold and feel   flight

a grasp at feathers

lapwing of now
dragged false

distracts me from tomorrow

what is it I flee

the sun glories so hot with arrows

the garden dies
even as it grows

scarlet-running of the beans opens to hummingbird whir

tomato blossoms' slim bells rung
by bees who look like boys

pulling bell ropes

feet leaving the ground

birds sleep in the moth clapped night

the centuries' fathers will not nest

only wander
among outcomes

this year all the women are wearing

native plants

I can only leave

a love letter to the light   closed
eyes pounding red lid blood

BE WHAT YOU SEE

the window is bay   glass she looks into

sand origin

through panes stirring

between house   garden

dropping hours   grain by stain

she forms weather

in shells collected on the sill

trouble

back when it was ordinary

a keep of pebbles

hurricane scored

betrays a wound of names

mankind and people she knows

she is stones

smatterings of a coast brought home

inlets curved by open seas alive

shivering with fish

she would be ocean   in outlaw drift

loving a sea monster

luring his haunches away from pole melt
taking his solitary paw   claw drawn
across the hottest days
she   a wide circle   of cooling skirts

in liminal glass   looks back

underwater at sand   beneath seas

where she turns in helixes of kelp   bubbling

by frangible lay of the littoral land

shoring up with the beast

having been   having seen

FIELD OF NOTES ///////// Dear Reader, The End

water fell with sidelines of slake love
ever runneling   someone died young
someone else lived to clear brush
on the other side   wing
breach   and of verdure
a woman's fields cast into net
tiny and the vast things caught
bodies of chitin and mane   angel
membrane   male cadences because
she is cicadas in the mirror   because she
is erasure surely of possible notes
brief bugs on a wire   landing

root androgyne   late grown she green-
antlering   woman-limbed offering
fiddleheads and honey
to guests who choose venison
cajole her into the evening's
cacophony   love creates its cost
granting years to deny   her rack
to cast off alliance   dalliance now
fixed for ghost trysts   eventual gusto

she secretes sweet to meat her hunter
sprocketed view of his twilight
so well-lit   so spackled   so held
by upholstery tacks   fabrications
and tactics   and so yes   she has been

in rut   bucks   does and archers
seek confluence of her origin streams
a childhood of omission   an X
she passes to them   preferring
to lie down on grassland
unable to extricate spine
from stalk   nerve from whole
classes of insect   hollow from vole
her enzyme from matrimony
what coupling is not doubling

endangered of her type they
will speak differently
of who she is   the body's piebald
world that should be a more womanly
accessory to garden   no crickets drying
in a box   touched by land she keeps
she knocks   blurs flesh at heaven carried
off toward sunset   cash bar extinction
where her trinket orb leaves its meadow
in the velvet ruin of her pocket

NOTES

WEDDING DRESSES BY ANSELM KIEFER is a poem about sculptures of wedding dresses created by the contemporary German artist Anselm Kiefer. They are (controversially) described by art critics as addressing the invisibility of women, and portraying the power of women. Kiefer claims this to be true.

In HOW YOU GET BACK HOME, the Valkyries come from old Norse mythology. Their name means 'chooser of the slain.' They are women, often on horseback, who decide which of the dead shall be admitted to Odin's Valhalla. Valhalla is a battlefield of fallen soldiers who come back to life at night to go drinking.

The opening quote and section title BEASTS LIVING IN THE MIRROR is taken from the title of a Jorge Luis Borges story, "Animals That Live in the Mirror," taken ostensibly from a Chinese myth about creatures imprisoned in the mirror. From *The Book of Imaginary Beings*, translated by Andrew Hurley.

FLOWER OF EMPIRE: THE TWO-NIGHT LIFE AND SEX CHANGE OF *VICTORIA AMAZONICA*, refers to a flower named for Queen Victoria. The lily pads grow to be up to ten feet in diameter. It was a popular photo opportunity for young women and girls to stand on the leaves. The public was obsessed with the flower and it came to represent the British Empire. A race ensued to bring the lily to England to flower. The flower is protogynous, meaning that the female reproductive organs mature before the male. As a female, the flower is white and fragrant. When it changes to male, it is red and scentless.

THE ART OF LOSING SUMMER title was inspired by a line of Elizabeth Bishop's in the poem "One Art," "the art of losing..."

NOMENCLATURE was inspired by *Werner's Nomenclature of Colours, Adapted To Zoology, Botany, Chemistry, Mineralogy, Anatomy, and the Arts,* by P. Syme, flower-painter, Edinburgh, 1821.

All colors in the poem NOMENCLATURE are my inventions, with the exception of 'gamboge,' from *Werner's Nomenclature.*

DEER WOMAN AS MELPOMENE, FACES THE MANIC COMEDY—Melpomene is one of the nine Greek muses, patron of tragedy. Thalia is the muse of comedy. They are opposites represented on the two masks of the theater, sad face and happy face.

ACKNOWLEDGMENTS

Grateful acknowledgment is made to the following journals where these poems first appeared, or are forthcoming in:

Bennington Review: "Be What You See," "Iron Dresses"

Best American Poetry Blog: "To the Animals Dreaming My Body," "Under Traveling Wildfire Haze"

Boston Review: "In a Time of Extinction," "Last Blush of My Chapped Planet," "Reap in Thunder Long"

Heavy Feather Review: "Woman's *Mappa Mundi* —The Promontory Imprint," "Where Did You Flee Without a Night"

Inverted Syntax: "Diary of Deer Woman," "Translate Us"

Lana Turner Journal: "Meadow of Corset," "Nomenclature"

The Laurel Review: "Reflection as Being in Lost Habitat"

Lily Poetry Review: "How You Get Back Home," "How to Grow Cover"

Massachusetts Review: "Heavenly Body Postmenopausal"

Ocean State Review: "Earthlock"

Poetry International: "Dear Survivor," "Nasturtiums"

Puerto Del Sol: "Flower of Empire: The Two-night Life and Sex Change of *Victoria Amazonica*"

Tupelo Quarterly: "Attend the Crowning Head," "Hem of Fire," "Queen Anne's Black Lace."

ABOUT THE AUTHOR

Photo: Jorg Meyer

Jenny Grassl is a poet and visual artist. Her poems have appeared in *Poetry International, Tupelo Quarterly, Bennington Review, Lana Turner Journal, Heavy Feather Review, Lit, The Grolier Prize Anthology, Ocean State Review, Laurel Review,* and others, including *The Boston Review* where she was a runner-up for the annual prize, selected by Mary Jo Bang. Her poetry was featured in a Best of American Poetry Blog. Her full-length collection, *Magicholia,* was published by 3: A Taos Press.

Her artwork has been exhibited widely, including at the Joyce Goldstein Gallery, Massachusetts, Fort Point Arts Community Gallery, Boston, Massachusetts, and Janapa Gallery, New York, New York. She creates images with poetry in a variety of media, including photography, digital collage, wood cut printmaking, and sculpture.

Jenny received her B.F.A. in photography from Rhode Island School of Design, her M.F.A. in creative writing, poetry, from Bennington Writing Seminars, and her soul degree from Lucie Brock-Broido's Sargent St. Workshop. Originally from Collegeville, Pennsylvania, she lives in Cambridge, Massachusetts.